This Journal Belongs

Printed Name

Autograph

My Life
My Journey

As you write your memoir journal, be sure to be as detailed and descriptive as possible. The more you paint the picture, the more authentic it will be, and the more your loved ones will enjoy your writings. You may not remember exact details, but your most accurate recollection is more than enough, because it is yours.

If there is anything that you think was missed in any of the sections, there is a "Notes" page at the end of each section for you to jot down any pertinent additional information.

contents

Introduction
Memories are priceless

Hello, and welcome to your guided journal. This journal was designed in hopes that families will have lasting memories from their cherished loved one for generations to come. Authoring this journal came about from losing family members and the realization that loved ones are getting older. Wanting to have some very basic, but intriguing questions answered by the ones we love the most was a must. The answers may seem mundane, but they will bring smiles to our faces for many years to come.

There are questions that will make you think a little. Nothing to personal, but personal enough, so we can read some things that we may have never known. It is a great conversation piece, it will get some laughs, maybe some tears, and for sure a lot of smiles. You can consider this a memoir, a commentary, or just a chronicle of your life's journey. Even if the memory has faded a bit, write your recollection from your heart, as memories are easily forgotten over the years, but still they are your memories.

Most of all, have fun with it and enjoy knowing you are leaving a small legacy of your life's journey. Your loved ones will cherish your writings forever...

Cheers and Enjoy...

Family Tree

_____
Great-Grandfather

_____
Great-Grandfather

_____
Great-Grandmother

_____
Great-Grandmother

_____
Grandmother

_____
Grandfather

_____
My Mother

_____
Me

_____
My Sibling

_____
My Sibling

_____
My Sibling

_____
My Sibling

_____
My Sibling

_____
My Sibling

_____
My Sibling

_____
My Sibling

Family Tree

_____
Great-Grandfather

_____
Great-Grandfather

_____
Great-Grandmother

_____
Great-Grandmother

_____
Grandmother

_____
Grandfather

_____
My Father

_____
My Grandchild

_____
My Significant Other

_____
My Grandchild

_____
My Child

_____
My Grandchild

_____
My Child

_____
My Grandchild

_____
My Child

_____
My Grandchild

_____
My Child

_____
My Grandchild

3

My Life My Journey

Notes

My Life My Journey
Welcome to the World

Welcome to the World is your life as a newborn. We all know that we do not really have memories from this time in our life, but we were told stories, watched old home movies, looked at pictures, and just laughed about it with our parents over the years. There have been plenty of smiles shared about you as that cute little baby, lets get them down on paper.

Do your best to put down what you have heard, seen, or been told. We all know it is probably just a guess or recollection, but we are all interested in how you got your start. This is the time when your parents and family said, Welcome to the World.

My Life My Journey
Welcome to the World

What is your full name and date of birth?

_____

_____

_____

_____

What city and state were you born?

_____

_____

_____

_____

What was the name of the hospital where you were born?

_____

_____

_____

_____

Were you named after anyone, is there any significance to your name?

_____

_____

_____

_____

_____

_____

My Life My Journey
Welcome to the World

What was your birth weight and height?

Do you remember the time of day you were born,
morning, afternoon, or night time?

How was labor for your mom when you were born?

How old were your parents when you were born?

My Life My Journey
Welcome to the World

Did you cry a lot as a baby?

_____
_____
_____
_____
_____

Did you go to preschool or have a babysitter? What do you remember about either?

_____
_____
_____
_____
_____
_____

Describe your first home or what you were told about where you lived as a newborn:

_____
_____
_____
_____
_____

My Life My Journey
Welcome to the World

Was there a lot of pictures and home movies of you as a baby?

Did you go see Santa, did you cry?

Did you have a favorite stuffed animal?

Were you bald or have a full head of hair as a newborn?

My Life My Journey

Notes

My Life My Journey
Elementary School Years

The elementary school years were some of the most fun years of our lives. Learning how to read and write, finding our way socially on the playground, doing chores around the house, we all had to find our way through these impressionable years. We may not remember every detail from them, but we remember our friends, how to color inside the lines, and the teachers that really had an impact on our young minds. The memories may be distant, but they are important to understanding how we grew up and became the person that we are today.

This may take a little thinking, but there will be a lot of smiles as you put the pen to paper. We were all there at one time, waiting to be excused from the lunch tables to go play, running across the playground, or just the anticipation of that first day of school. For the purposes of your journal we will consider elementary school years as kindergarten through 8th grade.

These are your elementary school years...

My Life My Journey
Elementary School Years

Name as many of your elementary school teachers as you can remember

---

What were the names of the elementary schools you attended?

My Life My Journey
Elementary School Years

Who was your favorite elementary school teacher, and why?

Who was your least favorite elementary school teacher, and why?

My Life My Journey
Elementary School Years

Who was your best friend in elementary school? How did you meet?

_____
_____
_____
_____
_____
_____

What was your favorite playground activity?

_____
_____
_____
_____
_____

Did you buy cafeteria lunch or take a sack lunch from home? Favorite lunch food?

_____
_____
_____
_____
_____

My Life My Journey
Elementary School Years

Did you ever get in any trouble in elementary school?

How did you get home from school; walk, bus, ride from parents?

What do you remember most about elementary school?

My Life My Journey
Elementary School Years

What kind of chores did you have as a kid?

Did you get an allowance as a kid? How much?

What did you spend your money on as a kid?

Did you collect anything as a kid?

My Life My Journey
Elementary School Years

Did you have a bicycle as a kid? What kind and color?

_____

_____

_____

_____

Did you have any pets during these early years?
Dog, cat, horse, what were their names?

_____

_____

_____

_____

_____

_____

_____

Who were some of your neighborhood friends?

_____

_____

_____

_____

_____

_____

_____

_____

My Life My Journey
Elementary School Years

Did you have to share a bedroom with any of your siblings?

Did your family sit at the table to eat dinner?

What were some of your favorite things to eat as a kid?

My Life My Journey
Elementary School Years

What were some of the best things about being a kid?

Most traumatic things from being a kid?

My Life My Journey

Notes

My Life My Journey
High School Years

The high school years are some of the most influential years of our lives. We learn how to manage time, start having multiple classes a day, and maybe start driving. We pretty much know it all as teenagers and along with all the added responsibility, there's acne, what a great time. There are awkward moments socially, some peer pressure, dances, and many other choices to be made, all in four years. You start off as the scared underclassmen, then slowly gain some traction, and soon enough you are the big senior on campus, and graduating.

For most, high school is the greatest time of their lives. You have some responsibility, but not all that comes along with being an "adult". It is a time of freedom and discovery. A moment in time that you look back and say, "I wanna go back". If only you could, but you can get some of the memories down on paper. The high school years section is from grades 9 through 12, make the memories last forever...

My Life My Journey
High School Years

What was the name of your high school, where, grad year?

What were your school colors?

What was your high school mascot?

Who was the Principal of your high school?

How many students were in your graduating class?

Who was President of the United States?

Did you have a car in high school? What was it?

Did you struggle with acne?

My Life My Journey
High School Years

Who was your best friend in high school? How did you meet?

Who were some other friends that you remember
hanging out with in high school?

What did you and your friends do for fun in high school?

My Life My Journey
High School Years

Did you have a high school sweetheart? What was their name?

How did you and your high school sweetheart start dating?

Did you go to your high school dances? Which ones?

My Life My Journey
High School Years

Which high school dance was the most fun? Why

What was your favorite subject in high school? Why?

What was your toughest subject in high school? Why?

My Life My Journey
High School Years

What high school teacher, coach, counselor, had the biggest impact on you, looking back?

_____
_____
_____
_____
_____
_____

Did you play any sports or extra curricular activities in high school?

_____
_____
_____
_____
_____

Did you have a job during high school? What was it?

_____
_____
_____
_____
_____

My Life My Journey
High School Years

Did you go on a senior trip or have a senior night? Where?

Who do you still keep in touch with from high school?

Did you experience any kind of peer pressure?

My Life My Journey
High School Years

Major historical event that happened during high school?

_____

_____

_____

_____

_____

_____

Does your high school have any famous alumni?

_____

_____

_____

_____

_____

_____

What would you do differently if you could go back to high school?

_____

_____

_____

_____

_____

_____

My Life My Journey
High School Years

What are some of your best memories from high school?

What are some or your not so good memories from high school?

My Life My Journey

Notes

My Life My Journey
On Your Own

This section of My Life, My Journey, lets delve into the years after you graduated high school. Whether you went off to college, went to the local college, moved out with friends, went into the military or stayed home and got a job. These guided questions will focus on those years you became an adult and started your journey in "the real world". This is when you started out trying to navigate life's road map, over the speed bumps, through the road blocks, and cruising in the fast lane, on your own.

Focus on how you felt and what you thought the future held for you. Most of us think we have the world by the tail, and nothing can stop us. We're free and we have all the answers. Well, lets see what these years had in store for you. You're On Your Own...

My Life My Journey

On your own

What did you think the future held, now that you were legal?

Did you register to vote? What political party did you register as?

**When you got out of high school did you
go to college, enlist in the military, get a job, or something else?**

My Life My Journey
On your own

What made you choose that particular
college, branch of the military, or job?

_____

_____

_____

_____

_____

_____

_____

Where did you live and how was that different than being at home?

_____

_____

_____

_____

_____

_____

_____

_____

Who were your roommates, and where were they from?

_____

_____

_____

_____

_____

_____

My Life My Journey
On your own

Were you homesick when you first went away?
What do you remember feeling being on your own?

_____

_____

_____

_____

_____

How was the food on your own, what did you know how to cook?

_____

_____

_____

_____

_____

What did you do for fun or entertainment?

_____

_____

_____

_____

My Life My Journey
On your own

What was your major, MOS, job, and for what years?

How often did you go home to see family? How was that?

Do you still keep in touch with anyone from this time of your life?

My Life My Journey

On your own

**Would you change anything about
what you decided to do out of high school?**

_____

_____

_____

_____

_____

_____

_____

_____

**If you could talk to your 18 year old self,
what advice would you give yourself?**

_____

_____

_____

_____

_____

_____

_____

_____

My Life My Journey

On your own

What are some of your best memories from this time?

What are some of your not so good memories from this time?

My Life My Journey

Notes

My Life My Journey
The Road You Traveled

The Road You Traveled section will get into a little of everything, from the early years to the present. This will give you and your loved ones an insight into how you have gotten to where you are today. This will be a genuine look into your journey, your dreams, where you have traveled, your accomplishments, your career and all that has shaped you along the way.

Make sure you write down everything and anything that comes to mind. We want to hear how bumpy or smooth the road you traveled was and how you became the incredibly unique person that you are today. Lets dive deep into the map of your life and see if we can relive where you came from and how you got here.

My Life My Journey
The Road You Traveled

Did you have a nickname growing up, if so how did you get it?

_____
_____
_____
_____
_____
_____

Where were some of the places you went on summer vacations with your parents?

_____
_____
_____
_____
_____
_____

What kind of pets have you had and what were their names?

_____
_____
_____
_____
_____
_____

My Life My Journey
The Road You Traveled

Growing up, what did you think you were going to do for a career?

What was your first job, and what was your wage?

What was your career and with what companies?

Can money buy happiness? Explain

_____
....
_____
....
_____
....
_____

Where was your best vacation ever?

_____
....
_____
....
_____
....
_____

What is your dream vacation?

_____
....
_____
....
_____
....
_____

My Life My Journey
The Road You Traveled

Have you been to any high school class reunions? How were they?

Who were some of your friends that showed up?

Who were some of your friends that didn't show up?

Were there any that had passed away?

What bones have you broken?

What surgeries have you had?

What health issues have you dealt with in your life?

My Life My Journey
The Road You Traveled

Where did your parents grow up and where does your family ancestry lead back to?

Describe your parents.

Describe your relationship with your parents. At 18 and now.

What are some personality traits you got from your parents?

What are some physical characteristics you got from your parents?

What are some family traditions you've carried on over the years?

My Life My Journey
The Road You Traveled

What is the greatest invention of your lifetime? Why

_____

_____

_____

_____

_____

_____

A big historical event do you vividly remember,
and where were you when it happened?

_____

_____

_____

_____

_____

What is or always has been your biggest fear?

_____

_____

_____

_____

_____

My Life My Journey
The Road You Traveled

What life lesson did you learn the hard way?

_____

_____

_____

_____

_____

What do you consider your biggest accomplishments?

_____

_____

_____

_____

_____

What are some of your biggest regrets?

_____

_____

_____

_____

_____

My Life My Journey
The Road You Traveled

If you could talk to one person from your past,
who would it be and what would you say?

If you could have dinner with one famous person,
who would it be, and why?

If you were President for a day,
what would you try and change?

My Life My Journey
The Road You Traveled

What are some of your biggest Pet Peeves?

What makes you laugh out loud?

What makes you cry?

Do you sing in the shower?

Differences growing up today, compared to when you grew up?

Has your life been different than what you imagined it would be?

How would you like to be remembered?

My Life My Journey

Notes

My Life My Journey
Love & Relationships

In our final section of our guided questions we will touch on love and relationships. The good, the sad, and the forever. Love is patient, love is kind, love is a big part of our journey. Love sometimes comes and finds us, and sometimes it seems like it is trying to hide. Relationships over the years will mold us and help us mature into sharing our lives with the love of our life.

Take this Love & Relationships section of your journal and dive deep into all the relationships that have shaped your life and your heart. This may spark some real emotion and we all want to learn a little from you and all of your experiences. Remember, the reason My Life, My Journey is in your hands right now, is because, You are Loved!!!

My Life My Journey
Love & Relationships

Do you believe in Love at first sight? Explain

How many times would you say, you've been in love?
How would you define love?

My Life My Journey
Love & Relationships

What is the most important thing in a loving relationship?

**What did you learn from past relationships
that helped you with the love of your life?**

How many times do you think you have been heartbroken?

What did you do to help ease the heartbreak?

What was the hardest part about relationships ending?

My Life My Journey
Love & Relationships

Where and how did you meet the love of your life?

What was your first impression of the love of your life?

My Life My Journey
Love & Relationships

How did the relationship start, with the love of your life?

_____

_____

_____

_____

_____

**Was the relationship always smooth,
or were there some bumps in the road?**

_____

_____

_____

_____

_____

When and where did you get married?

_____

_____

_____

_____

_____

My Life My Journey
Love & Relationships

What is your favorite memory with the love of your life?

What is their best quality?

What did you learn most from the love of your life?

My Life My Journey

Notes

My Life My Journey
Favorites

A lot of the time people can tell a lot from what your favorite movie is or who your favorite President was. The Favorites section is just that, a quick "what is your favorite", group of questions. Put down the first thing that comes to mind. Most of these questions should spark an instant answer as soon as you read it. You've accomplished a lot getting your answers on paper to this point of your journal. These questions should be pretty simple and fun.

My Life My Journey
Favorites

Favorite Movie?

Favorite TV show?

Favorite band and song?

Favorite actor or actress?

Favorite food and drink?

Favorite President?

Favorite season of the year?

Favorite holiday?

My Life My Journey
Favorites

Favorite Dessert?

Favorite State you've visited?

Favorite animal?

Favorite day of the week?

Favorite hobby?

Favorite Super Hero?

Favorite restaurant?

Favorite color?

My Life My Journey

Notes

My Life My Journey
18 vs Now

This should be a lot of fun. 18 vs Now is to compare what prices were around the time you were graduating from high school compared to the present. We don't need to be scientific, we all know that the cost of inflation has gone up dramatically. It will be a fun way to show younger generations how much things used to cost. They will be blown away and will for sure get a good laugh. You can look up prices from the that year or you can just take an guess. Have some fun and lets delve into your past wallet.

My Life My Journey
18 vs Now

What was the cost of the following when you were 18

Year: _____

Gallon of Gasoline _____

 Gallon of Milk _____

Your childhood home _____

Your First Car _____

First Class Postage Stamp _____

McDonalds Hamburger _____

Cup of Coffee _____

Movie Ticket _____

Haircut _____

Dozen Eggs _____

My Life My Journey
18 vs Now

What was the cost of the following when you were 18

Year: _____

Loaf of Bread   _____

Minimum Wage   _____

1 lb of ground beef   _____

TV   _____

Pair of Shoes   _____

Domestic Flight   _____

Newspaper   _____

Box of Cereal   _____

Washing Machine   _____

Bicycle   _____

My Life My Journey

Notes

My Life My Journey
This or That

This or That is a fun section to see what you would choose between two common things. It may surprise your loved ones at what you choose, but it will be fun to let then know that you prefer, Coke over Pepsi, or vice versa.

Sometimes you can really tell a person from what they choose in a quick read, This or That. Have some fun and circle whatever strikes your fancy first.

My Life My Journey
This or That

Dog	or	Cat
Cake	or	Pie
Wake Up Early	or	Sleep In
Batman	or	Superman
Pancake	or	Waffle
Coke	or	Pepsi
Coffee	or	Tea
Beach	or	Mountains
Target	or	Walmart
Beer	or	Wine
TV Shows	or	Movies

My Life My Journey

This or That

4' Feet Tall	or	8' Feet Tall
Know it all	or	Have it all
Rich & Unhealthy	or	Poor & Healthy
Live in Iran	or	Live in Siberia
Able to Fly	or	Turn Invisible
Stop Crime	or	Stop Pollution
Sleep, TV On	or	Sleep, TV Off
Sunset	or	Sunrise
Book Smart	or	Street Smart
Back to the Past	or	Forward to the Future
Comedy Movie	or	Thriller Movie

My Life My Journey

Notes

My Life My Journey
Bucket List

This was made famous by a 2007 movie where two complete strangers want to complete a list of things that they have always wanted to see and do before it's too late. Now people are putting their "Bucket List" down on paper and seeing if they can check some items of those items off. Everyone should have a Bucket List.

What were some things you've always wanted to see or do? Is it going on a safari, vacationing in Paris, skydiving, taking a family picture or something as simple as writing a journal about your life's journey? Only you can answer, what is on your Bucket List.

My Life My Journey

Bucket List

My Life My Journey

Bucket List

My Life My Journey
Notes to my loved ones

The following pages are for you to take some time and write some notes to your loved ones. Just a little something to the people that care about you and have loved you along your journey. A quick little "I Love You" means so much to the ones you love. It can be a general, to all my grandchildren, I love you and you have made me so proud. Or it can be quite detailed to a specific person that has been a big part of your life's journey, it is all up to you. Let them know, you love them and that they have mattered along way. They are part of My Life, My Journey...

My Life My Journey

Notes to my loved ones

My Life My Journey

Notes to my loved ones

My Life My Journey

Notes to my loved ones

My Life My Journey

Notes to my loved ones

My Life My Journey

Notes to my loved ones

My Life My Journey

Notes to my loved ones

My Life My Journey

My Life My Journey

Thank you for taking the time to complete your guided journal of your life's journey. I hope it was insightful and will bring many years of happiness and smiles to your family and loved ones. Most of all I hope that it gives you a sense that you are leaving a legacy for all those that really love and care about you.

Feel free to recommend a journal for all your loved ones and close friends. This journal is designed to make it easy for loved ones to share memories and have their legacy live on for generations. Thank you for writing My Life, My Journey...

Made in United States
Troutdale, OR
12/02/2024

25759862R00053